All About
Benjamin Franklin

Elizabeth Zuckerman

BLUE RIVER PRESS

Indianapolis, Indiana

All About Benjamin Franklin

Published by Blue River Press
Indianapolis, Indiana
www.brpressbooks.com

Distributed by Cardinal Publishers Group
Tom Doherty Company, Inc.
www.cardinalpub.com

ISBN: 978-1-68157-092-1

Author: Elizabeth Zuckerman
Series Editor: Charleen Davis
Editor: Dani McCormick
Interior Illustrator: Molly Dykstra
Cover Artist: Jennifer Mujezinovic
Cover Design: David Miles
Book Design: Dave Reed

Printed in the United States of America

Contents

Young Ben Franklin could only imagine
how he would change history

All About
Benjamin Franklin

Preface

Ben Franklin was one of America's greatest Founding Fathers: a printer, scientist, and statesman who shaped the fate of our country. Born into a working-class family, he made his way with wits and talent rather than money and connections. His discoveries and inventions made him a celebrity in his own time. Queens and lords recognized his face as easily as we do today. For many people, then and now, he embodies the best of American ingenuity, spirit, and cleverness.

But Ben never wanted the spotlight. At an early age, he decided that the best way to live was not by being admired, but by being useful. Where other people would shake their heads in despair, Ben could always find a new and creative solution in arenas ranging from politics to science to indoor heating. He built his many successful careers by finding new and better ways to improve life, whether by starting his own business, protecting houses from fire and lightning, or even by championing an infant nation as it struggled to find its place in the world. If he believed in a cause, he never stopped fighting for it.

Philadelphia, a relatively young city, had a booming economy and plenty of opportunities for a young man like Ben to make a name for himself

During his lifetime, which spanned eighty-four of America's most turbulent years, Ben was always on the front lines of change. At seventeen, he ran away to the fastest growing city in his homeland, Philadelphia. His experiments with electricity challenged the accepted wisdom of the time. He saw thirteen colonies defy the greatest army Europe had to offer, and did all he could to help them succeed. By doing so, he and the other Founding Fathers put their lives in danger. If the American Revolution had failed, Ben and his fellow rebels would have been executed as traitors to the English crown. To Ben, the risk was worth it to do the right thing.

Benjamin Franklin was one of the country's memorable Founding Fathers

Not only was he brave, but he was also a visionary thinker. He spoke out against slavery and prejudice against Native Americans. His witty quips, which based their jokes in human nature, are as true today as they were when he wrote them. He founded dozens of organizations, many of which are still active today. And the country for which he worked so tirelessly has only admired him more with time. From fire departments to libraries to universities, from student scholarships to nationally recognized centers of scientific learning, Ben's legacy continues to shape America, more than two centuries after his death.

This popular painting of Ben is the most recognizable
because it was chosen for the $100 bill

Chapter One
Growing Up

America in 1706 was not yet a country, but a set of territories called colonies, populated by English settlers and loosely connected by their loyalty to England. The oldest English colony was Virginia, founded ninety-nine years earlier in 1607. Twenty-one years after Virginia was founded, the Puritans founded the Massachusetts Bay colony. Ben Franklin was born in Boston, Massachusetts's largest city, in 1706.

Ben's father, Josiah, had been born in England, and came to Boston in 1682 with his wife Anne and three children. After Anne died in childbirth with their seventh child, Josiah married Ben's mother, Abiah Folger. Josiah was the first in his family to come to America, but Abiah's father had been one of New England's first settlers. Ben was their eighth child, the youngest son, and with only two sisters after him, the third-youngest Franklin. Josiah and Anne's second son had died in infancy, but all the other young Franklins—nine boys and seven girls—grew to adulthood.

At age sixty-five, Ben could remember thirteen Franklin children gathered around the dinner table at one time. Of his many siblings, Ben was closest with his sister Jane, born six years after him and the youngest of his siblings. Both Ben and Jane had very fond memories of their childhood and of their parents, who worked very hard to feed and care for their children.

A huge family like the Franklins would have been hopelessly crowded in England, where the lands were already settled and the jobs already taken. In the American colonies, which English settlers had occupied for less than a century, there was plenty of room for each Franklin son to learn his own trade. Girls in this day learned housekeeping by helping their mothers with the never-ending work of keeping up a house, but boys typically were apprenticed to a local tradesman or learned from their fathers.

Josiah Franklin, who encouraged his children to be honest, thoughtful, and hard-working, required each of his sons to learn a useful business. His fourth son John followed in his father's footsteps and became a candle maker, or chandler; James, the sixth son, had a printing shop. Ben himself went to school at age eight because Josiah hoped that Ben would become a churchman. Ben loved reading and soon rose to the top of his class, but the school was too expensive, and his father brought him home to

Ben loved reading as a child and quickly exhausted his father's small library

learn the family trade of candle making when Ben was ten years old.

Chandlers were very important before electrical lighting and worked long hours in hot conditions

Chandlers worked long and tedious hours over large vats of hot wax and tallow. When they weren't pouring the tallow into molds, they were sweating over pots of it boiling down into soap. Although he loved his father, Ben didn't like the job. He would much rather have gone to sea.

Ben had learned to swim when he was very young, and even attached paddles to his hands and feet to swim more easily. He was enchanted by the water and ships, but his father wouldn't hear of Ben going to sea. He thought being a sailor was a dangerous and frivolous life. When Ben started to show interest in becoming a sailor, his father quickly took him around to every tradesman in Boston, hoping that Ben would find some other trade to pursue.

Ben could never remember a time when he couldn't read. He devoured his father's small library before he was ten, reading popular books like *Pilgrim's Progress* and essays by the great Puritan preacher Cotton Mather. Once he finished those, he had to get creative if he wanted to read anything new. Although there were printers in the American colonies, all the best books had to be imported at great expense from England. When Ben had a little money of his own, he loved to buy books, and would often resell books he'd already read in order to buy new ones. He even taught Jane to read and write so that his favorite sister could enjoy the same books he did.

His love of reading finally made Josiah Franklin decide that Ben should be apprenticed to his brother James, the printer, so that he could always be surrounded by books. Ben still wanted to go to sea, but he finally signed an apprenticeship agreement with his brother when he was twelve-years-old. Few boys chose their own careers; they either learned a trade from their father, or, like Ben, had one picked for them.

Apprenticeship in 1718, when Ben was twelve, was a serious business contract. Masters like James, who ran their own businesses, trained apprentices through childhood into adulthood. Apprentices did all the heaviest or dullest work and moved up to more challenging assignments as they got better, so that by the end of their apprenticeship, they knew the business inside-and-out. In return, masters fed, clothed, and housed their apprentices.

But not all masters were good teachers. Some resented skilled apprentices who were better craftsmen than the masters themselves, so they wouldn't promote them to the more interesting work. Some cut costs by not giving their apprentices good food, or even enough food. Others just weren't very good at their jobs in the first place, so their apprentices didn't learn anything useful.

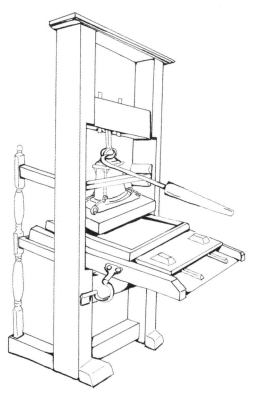

Printing presses of the day could only print one page at a time and required careful preparation

Ben considered himself lucky that he would learn from his own brother. He soon found out that James had other ideas. In 1718, James was twenty-one. He had started his own printing business only a year before. Though he was a good printer, he was a newcomer and had a lot to prove.

Ben, as the apprentice, often had to do the hard work while his brother did less difficult tasks

Ben assumed that he would be treated as James's brother. James preferred to think of Ben only as his apprentice and assigned him not only boring jobs, but lowly ones too. He also beat Ben. Masters often beat their apprentices, but Ben had expected to be spared that from his own brother. Ben felt like a servant, and certainly not like a brother. Worse, his apprenticeship lasted for nine years, until he himself would be twenty-one. He hated the thought of spending nine years at James's mercy.

The brothers often argued over James's treatment of Ben. Whenever they couldn't settle a fight between them, they took the argument to their father. Josiah heard both sides equally, but when he sided with Ben, James would beat Ben even worse. His apprenticeship was Ben's first lesson in tyranny. But if James was a harsh master, he was also a good teacher.

Printing was a complicated job in the eighteenth century. Every page to be printed had to be laid out from top to bottom, using tiny individual letters cut out of small metal blocks. The letters were called moveable type, because you could move them anywhere you wanted on the page. A good printer needed thousands of letters in many different sizes. They all had to be kept clean and organized. What made it even trickier was that the letters were all backwards!

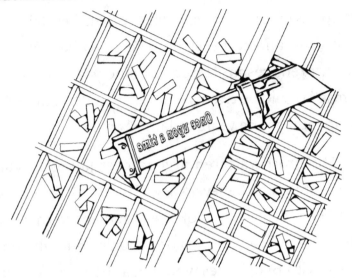

Moveable type used individually carved letters to create pages for the press

Once a page was laid out, with all its words spelled backwards, the type would be coated with ink. The ink had to be put on evenly, to avoid great black blotches on the finished page. Then the page would be placed on the press itself, and a clean sheet of paper put on top of the inked letters. Finally, the printer would press down on the paper, using a printing machine called a press to make sure that all the pressure was evenly distributed and the paper didn't wrinkle. The backwards type would transfer forwards onto the page!

But even then the job wasn't done. Every printed page had to be hung up safely out of the way while the ink dried. Only the next day would the page be ready for the customer. Everything was printed this way, from single-page fliers to be handed out on the street, to books with several hundred pages. A good printer could print dozens of pages every day.

And James was a good printer. Ben worked hard from morning to night, sorting and cleaning type and hanging printed pages to dry. As long as there was light to see by, James kept Ben at work. Ben quickly learned the ins-and-outs of a printing shop, but his favorite part of his apprenticeship was how easily he could get more books. If he promised to return a book the next morning, clean and free of stains, he could borrow it from Boston's booksellers, who did business with James. Soon Ben was working all day and reading all night. All this reading made him eager to refine his own writing, which he was already trying to improve by comparing it with articles in an English newspaper, the *Spectator*.

Ben's workload got heavier in 1721, when James started America's first independent newspaper, the *New England Courant*. Not only did Ben arrange the type and print off the paper's pages, but he also had to carry copies to the paper's subscribers, as well as selling extras in the Boston streets. It cost four pennies per copy, which made it the most expensive paper of its day.

Some of James's friends, who didn't think the paper would do well, had tried to persuade James not to print it, but other friends wrote witty articles and letters to help establish the *Courant*. James often printed such pieces, because he knew it made people want to buy the paper. But none of James's friends had sat awake at night with a candle and a copy of the *Spectator*, puzzling out what made a piece of writing good or bad. By the spring of 1722, Ben, sixteen and ambitious for more than James grudgingly allowed, knew his chance had come.

However, he also knew that James, who considered him a lowly apprentice instead of a brother

Ben was known for his great printing skills and his
ability to work quickly and efficiently

and equal, would never print Ben's writing if he
knew who wrote it. So Ben created a pseudonym.
He slipped a letter under the door of James's print
shop, supposedly written by a widow named Silence
Dogood. The letter was full of personality and a
little prideful, but most importantly, it was funny.

On April 2, 1722, James published it in the *New England Courant*.

Encouraged, Ben wrote more letters as Silence Dogood. He invented a whole history for his imaginary pen name, and used the persona to make wry comments on life in Boston. Every other week, he would slip a letter under the print shop door. His writing was so believable that several men wrote to the *Courant* offering to marry Silence Dogood!

In the summer of 1722, publishing Silence Dogood's letters got easier for Ben. James, who was never shy about expressing his opinion, had written several articles in the *Courant* that criticized the government of Boston. As a punishment, James was actually imprisoned for four weeks, and had to rely on Ben to print the *Courant* regularly. Not only did this make it easier for Ben to add his writing to the paper, but it gave him even more experience as a printer now that he had to run the print shop himself. When an extra punishment was added after James's release—that the *Courant* couldn't be printed under his name anymore—James was forced to put Ben's name on the paper instead, although

James took over the important tasks again, and treated Ben just as badly as he had before.

Running the *Courant* showed Ben that he could handle the responsibility of running a press by himself without the guidance of James

After this brief freedom, things only got worse between Ben and James. Ben enjoyed getting credit for the hard work he did on his brother's paper, but James felt that Ben had tried to steal the *Courant* from him. Ben resented that James still treated him like a lowly apprentice and didn't trust him to do things right, even after he'd run the paper for a month on his own. Worst of all, James soon discovered that Ben was Silence Dogood. Furious at being tricked by his little brother, James became even harsher.

Ben was now seventeen, with four more years to go on his apprenticeship. He had signed a contract and couldn't legally break it, but the thought of spending four more years doing dull and unimportant work for James was intolerable. Even more than that, he believed in his own talent and intelligence. He knew his thoughts and dreams were bigger than James's, and he longed to strike out on his own, which James would never let him do. Even Josiah was now on James's side, for leaving an apprenticeship meant breaking your word.

There was only one choice that Ben could stand. It would be dangerous, but even risk was better than being trapped. He talked a friend into secretly getting him passage on a boat leaving Boston, packed what little he owned, and ran away. He was now a fugitive from the law, a teenager running out

Ben ran away to Philadelphia,
more than 300 miles away from Boston

on his apprenticeship, and he could be arrested and dragged back home if anyone recognized him. Now he was free and in control of his own life for the first time. And he was headed to Philadelphia, the most exciting city in all the colonies.

Chapter Two
Philadelphia and London

Philadelphia was as different from Boston as night is from day. Boston was one of the oldest European cities in North America, founded by a strict Puritan religious sect, and already too established for a bright and ambitious young man like Ben to make much impact. On the other hand, Philadelphia was sixty years younger than Boston and growing faster than it had room for. Its Quaker founder, William Penn, had welcomed people from all nations and all religions to make a home there.

Many different kinds of people found their way to Philadelphia: peaceful, easygoing Quakers, immigrants hoping for a better life, and energetic thinkers like Ben who wanted a place where their ideas could take root. To top it all off, Philadelphia was one of the major trading ports with England. Anyone and anything could be found in Philadelphia!

Ben was excited to have arrived, and hopeful that his printing skills would get him a good job. But when he got off the boat, after a rough trip which thoroughly cured him of wanting to be a sailor, he could think only of how hungry he felt. Unfortunately, he had barely any money. He stopped at a bakery and asked for however much bread three pennies—less than the cost of a copy of the *New England Courant* in Boston—would buy him.

To his shock and delight, the baker promptly handed him three enormous puffy rolls. Ben had grown so used to scanty food that this was more than enough. With all his extra clothes stuffed in his pockets, he had nowhere to carry the delicious rolls. He ended up putting one roll under each arm and stuffing the third in his mouth to eat as he walked. Ben's clothes were battered from the sea voyage and carrying the rolls made it hard to walk down the street. He certainly made a strange sight to young Deborah Read, who was standing at her door when Ben waddled by. She could not help but giggle, and she was so charming that Ben couldn't help but notice her.

In 1723, there were two rival printers in Philadelphia—Andrew Bradford and Samuel Keimer. Brad-

Deborah Read saw Ben for the first time in 1723 as he waddled down the street, overloaded with bread

ford had enough help, so Ben went to work for Keimer. He soon found out that Keimer barely knew a thing about good printing; his equipment was old and outdated, and he wasted time by composing his articles with the type instead of writing it out on paper first. Ben was not impressed with him or with Bradford, but they were the only printers in town. Besides, as well as employing him, Keimer found him a place to live. And as luck would have it, it was the same house where Deborah Read lived. As her parents' boarder, or paying houseguest, Ben could spend as much time with her as he wanted.

Of course, he didn't have a lot of free time to flirt. He quickly made several friends among the other young men of Philadelphia who loved to read as much as he did. They critiqued each other's writing to help each other improve. Keimer soon relied on Ben for everything, but Ben himself wasn't content to play second fiddle to a bad printer.

Ben's second cousin had put him in touch with William Keith, the governor of Pennsylvania, who wanted Ben to set up shop for himself. Keith not only reconciled Ben's family to his living in Philadelphia, but promised to send Ben to London to get a state-of-the-art press, and to become his customer when he returned.

Ben traveled to London to buy a printing press
with his friend James Ralph

Trusting in Keith's word, Ben made ready to sail
to London, the largest, most exciting, and most
important city in the English-speaking world. Before he left, he proposed to Deborah. But Deborah's mother didn't want her daughter marrying a
seventeen-year-old apprentice with no business,
who wouldn't even be in Philadelphia for the fore-
seeable future. Although Ben and Deborah loved
each other, Mrs. Read forbade them to marry. So
Ben sailed for England over winter seas with only his
friend James Ralph and the letters of recommenda-
tion and credit that Governor Keith had promised
him.

Unfortunately, when he got to London, he found that these were not only worthless, but not even from Governor Keith. The governor, he realized, was wonderful at promising, but terrible at delivering. At eighteen-years-old, Ben found himself in a strange city, across the ocean from his birthplace, with no chance of buying a good printing press and only his wits to support him.

Ben found work at Palmer's, a famous London print shop. He and Ralph lived together to save money, but the expense of London, and going out at night, meant that they spent almost as much as they made. To make matters worse, Ben and Ralph argued after Ralph had borrowed a lot of money, and the severed friendship prevented Ben from getting his money back.

Rather than give up, Ben treated the loss of his friend as a wake-up call to make the most out of his time in London. He went to Watts', an even more famous print shop, and astonished his fellow workers by refusing to drink the huge amounts of beer that they did. He preferred water, having seen that drinking too much beer made his companions slow and weak. Since they thought that beer made them strong, they could make no sense out of the fact that Ben, whom they called "the water-American," could carry twice as much as they could. Eventually Ben convinced some of them to give up beer for healthier (and cheaper) food, and even made a little extra money by lending a few pennies with interest to the rest who still wanted beer.

His coworkers regularly drank beer
while working, but Ben stuck to water

Although he enjoyed London, Ben did not want to stay there forever. Just as in Boston, the print shops were already established, and in spite of his experience and skills, it was much harder to make his way in London than in Philadelphia. Luckily, a Quaker friend of his hired him to help with his business. In July of 1726, they sailed back to Philadelphia.

Ben sails for home in the Berkshire,
a three-masted schooner, in 1726

Ben had been gone almost two years. His time in London had increased his fondness and respect for England, the mother country of the American colonies. It had also shown him that despite his talent and ambition, he had made bad decisions. There was still plenty of work to be done on his character before he could be happy with himself. And there was no time like the present to start.

While at sea, Ben wrote one of his most famous pieces. It was a plan for living well and happily by following thirteen "virtues" like justice, sincerity, and humility. He resolved to live by this plan for the rest of his life. He would focus on one virtue for a week, to get himself into the habit. The next week, he would switch to another virtue. Later in life, he lamented that he never perfected any of them, but stated that the effort had made him much happier than he would have been if he had never tried!

Ben Franklin's Thirteen Virtues

1. Temperance: Eat not to dullness, drink not to elevation.

2. Silence: Speak not but what may benefit others or yourself. Avoid trifling conversation.

3. Order: Let all your things have their places. Let each part of your business have its time.

4. Resolution: Resolve to perform what you ought. Perform without fail what you resolve.

5. Frugality: Make no expense but to do good to others or yourself: i.e., waste nothing.

6. Industry: Lose no time. Be always employed in something useful. Cut off all unnecessary actions.

7. Sincerity: Use no hurtful deceit. Think innocently and justly; and, if you speak, speak accordingly.

8. Justice: Wrong none by doing injuries or omitting the benefits that are your duty.

9. Moderation: Avoid extremes. Forbear resenting injuries so much as you think they deserve.

10. Cleanliness: Tolerate no uncleanness in body, clothes or habitation.

11. Tranquility: Be not disturbed at trifles, or at accidents common or unavoidable.

12. Chastity: Rarely use venery but for health or offspring; never to dullness, weakness, or the injury of your own or another's peace and reputation.

13. Humility: Imitate Jesus and Socrates.

Chapter Three
<u>Striking Out</u>

Ben returned to Philadelphia determined to make himself a new man. Armed with his list of virtues and his London-trained experience, he went back to work for Keimer, who had finally gotten a better press and some new apprentices. To Ben's delight, they were all about his age, and almost as smart as Ben himself. Not so pleasant was the realization that Keimer was only using Ben to train the new apprentices, after which Keimer would no longer need Ben.

Luckily, Ben's hard work and good teaching made the apprentices respect him more than Keimer. Some of them got along so well that they arranged meetings every Friday to hold spirited debates about moral issues and the search for truth. Ben called this fledgling society the Junto, and selected its members very carefully. His resolution to improve himself made him pick fellow thinkers who were also interested in self-improvement; he didn't want anyone lazy or careless in his club.

The Junto society gathered regularly to discuss philosophy, morality, ethics, and truth

There were twelve original members, who came from all the walks of life that bustling Philadelphia could offer. They included a mathematician, a shoemaker, a surveyor, a cabinet-maker, a wealthy gentleman, and the three best of Keimer's apprentices, as well as three other men. Every week they chose topics to write and talk about for next week, and even shared their precious books to help everyone understand the subjects more. Although Ben was only twenty-one, he was the Junto's unquestioned leader.

While the Junto satisfied Ben's mind, his professional ambitions continued to be thwarted by Keimer's jealousy. Keimer resented paying him proper wages, and became even more tyrannical than James had been. The break finally came when Keimer picked a fight with Ben in public, which ended in Ben getting fired. With no job and not enough money to start his own business, Ben thought with despair of going back to Boston. It was not a pleasant prospect. Although his family had accepted his running away, Ben had still broken a serious professional promise.

The thought of returning to his father's disapproval without any success to show for his rebellion horrified him. And of course, time had not stopped for the Franklins in Boston. At age fifteen, his sister Jane had just married Edmund Mecom, a saddler who couldn't afford a house of his own. Ben's already-crowded childhood home was even more crowded with Jane and her husband living there. Worst of all, James still held a grudge, and wouldn't allow Ben to work in Boston.

To his surprise, his friend Hugh Meredith, an apprentice and a member of the Junto, came up with a plan. Hugh hated the idea of Ben leaving, and reminded him that Keimer's printing business was in debt. A bad printer and a worse businessman, Keimer was doomed to failure, which would open up a chance for a good printer in Philadelphia. And Hugh's father, who thought well of Ben, would give them the money they needed to get started. Newly hopeful, Ben agreed to a partnership with Hugh,

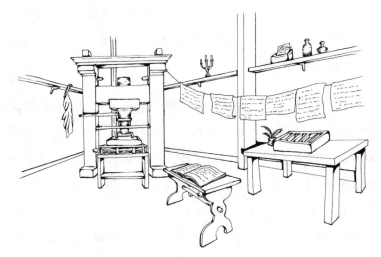

Ben's print shop in Philadelphia
was small but successful

and they ordered their new state-of-the-art equipment from London, while Hugh served out the last few months of his apprenticeship before Keimer got wind of the plan. In 1728, Ben and Hugh opened Philadelphia's newest print shop.

They got their first job through the Junto. A Quaker member commissioned them to print forty pages of a Quaker history. Hugh, while truly friendly and well-meaning, was not a very dedicated worker, so Ben ran the entire shop, and soon bought him out with the help of two close friends.

He knew that this first job could make or break his professional reputation, so it had to be perfect. His hard work on the Quaker history made people think very well of him, not just personally, but as a professional. The quality of Ben's printing was beyond compare in Philadelphia, and very soon he began to get all the important and well-paying jobs.

Knowing how important public perception was to his fledgling business, he cultivated a reputation as a diligent worker, wheeling large wagons loaded with heavy goods down the street by himself in a combined publicity stunt and workout. He was even able, in 1729, to buy out the little newspaper that Keimer had started. This paper, the *Pennsylvania Gazette*, would become one of his most famous legacies. It stayed in print until 1800, ten years after Ben's death, and would print America's first political cartoon (which Ben himself drew) in 1754.

As part of a publicity stunt, Ben wheeled heavy wheelbarrows down the street

November 10. 1748.

The Pennfylvania *GAZETTE.*

NUMB. 1039.

Containing the frefbeft Ad- *vices, Foreign and Domeftick.*

MERCY JUSTICE

The Pennsylvania Gazette was one of Ben's favorite projects and published articles on many topics, but mostly politics

It was a good time for Ben. Not only was he succeeding professionally, he had reconnected with Deborah Read. While he was in London, she had been pressured into marrying a ne'er-do-well named John Rogers, who had run off with most of her dowry around 1727.

Ben had been too embarrassed to visit Deborah again after his return, feeling that she might not have been forced into this unhappy marriage if he had stayed in Philadelphia. But their friends soon assured him that Deborah still loved him. When Ben plucked up his courage and visited Deborah at last, she welcomed him back with open arms. And as Philadelphia's newest businessman and the talk of the town, not even Mrs. Read could deny that he was now a very promising match. Ben and Deborah started their new life together on September 1, 1730, along with Ben's newborn son William. Nothing about William's birth is certain except for the fact that Ben was his father. His mother may have been Deborah, or another woman whose name has been lost to history. What is certain is that Deborah and William always thought of each other as mother and son.

Benjamin and Deborah Franklin hold
Ben's first son William in 1731

In fact, William spent his early childhood more with Deborah than with Ben, who worked long hours. Eighteenth-century children grew up quickly, as a young child William stayed home, learning from Deborah to read and write—essential knowledge for a printer's son.

Although Deborah herself had not had much formal education, she knew enough to manage the bookstore Ben soon attached to his print shop, and she and Ben wrote each other diligently when they were apart. Two years old when his brother Francis was born, William would have been expected to help watch his baby brother, although he was still a baby by modern standards.

Chapter Four
Ventures

For anyone else, personal and professional success would have been more than enough. But Ben's active mind could never stop looking for ways to improve the quality of life, or to make bad systems good. Although the Junto's lending library hadn't worked the way they had hoped, Ben still believed the idea was good. Along with several friends from the Junto, he drew up a plan for a city-wide library in 1731. It cost forty shillings to join, a substantial although not huge sum, but less than it would have cost to import books from England.

Wary of seeming to back only his own plans, Ben explained idea of the library to several possible subscribers as the idea of a group of people who wanted to improve literacy in the colonies. The library was a hit, and continues to flourish to this day as the Library Company of Philadelphia.

Ben learned a lesson from this venture that he would apply to every project he undertook from then on. It was better, he found, to sacrifice his vanity and be committed to the idea itself than to claim it as his own and seem like a glory hound. After all, he reasoned, it didn't matter how or under whose name a good and useful idea became a reality. If it was good and useful, the most important thing was making it happen, not taking the credit.

Ben started Philadelphia's library in 1731, which became the basis for many public libraries

While Ben certainly encouraged this image of himself as a disinterested champion of improvement, it wasn't just an image, but the truth at the heart of all his public service. He even found that by stepping back and letting other people shine, his fellow citizens liked him more, which of course made it easier to get their support for his next project!

Luckily, he didn't need help for his newest plan. In 1732, he began to print an almanac, using his second pseudonym, or fake name: Richard Saunders. Almanacs were the 1700s' version of the weather forecast, combined with a calendar. Based on weather patterns from previous years, a good almanac could predict the best days to plant crops or to set sail. It was often also the only calendar widely available to colonists. Ben's almanac was unique. Not only did it contain all the important data that Philadelphians needed, it included several short and witty pieces of advice.

The almanac, soon called *Poor Richard's Almanac* after Ben's pseudonym, made Ben a rich man. The short and witty advice was very popular. We still use some of the most famous ones today! "A stitch in time saves nine" reminds us that it's better to do a little work now than a lot later. "A friend in need is a friend indeed" points out that real friends will support you when you need them, not just when it's easy for them. And anyone who's had a guest stay too long knows the truth: "Fish and visitors stink after three days."

Poor Richard, 1733.

A N

Almanack

For the Year of Christ

1733,

Being the First after LEAP YEAR:

And makes since the Creation	Years
By the Account of the Eastern *Greeks*	7241
By the Latin Church, when ☉ ent. ♈	6932
By the Computation of *W.W.*	5742
By the *Roman* Chronology	5682
By the *Jewish* Rabbies	5494

Poor Richard's Almanac was incredibly popular and helped provide Ben with a steady income so he could explore new projects

With money from *Poor Richard's Almanac* coming in, Ben didn't have to work so hard. At last he had a little free time to do things simply because they interested him. He and Deborah celebrated the birth of another son, Francis, who sadly died four years later of smallpox. Ben took up chess, becoming in 1733 the first American chess player on record. He taught himself French, Italian, and Spanish. Concerned about the easy spread of fires from wooden house to wooden house, he founded

Ben taught himself to play the European game of chess and, in 1733, became the first American to do so

the Union Fire Company, the first firefighting institution in America.

Ben started a partnership with Louis Timothy, a young man he trained and sent to South Carolina, to set up another branch of the *Pennsylvania Gazette*. Later, when Timothy died, his widow Elizabeth maintained the partnership so well that she eventually bought Ben out. Impressed by her business skills, Ben recommended that all girls receive education in finance so that they could take care of themselves if they had to.

Giving some thought to improvement, Ben proposed a huge change to the Junto. It had become more than just a club to Ben; he saw it as the incubator for his new ideas, as well as the birthplace of several close friendships. He knew he wasn't the only person in Philadelphia interested in changes for the better who could benefit from a serious intellectual organization. He suggested that its members each form a new club based on the Junto, without telling the new members about the original club. That way the Junto could reach a wider audience without having to alter itself. Not only did this plan work, but it widened the network of all members, both original and new, and made it easier to get public support for new projects.

As clerk for the Pennsylvania Assembly,
Ben recorded all of the meetings
and helped make important decisions

In 1736, the same year that little Francis died, Ben was made clerk, or secretary, of the Pennsylvania Assembly. The Assembly was the lawmaking body of the colony, reporting to the governor and to the descendants of William Penn, who had founded Pennsylvania. As clerk, Ben sat in on all their debates and decisions, recorded all the discussions and decisions of each meeting, and could even bring up ideas of his own. The next year, he became the postmaster for Philadelphia, which meant he was in charge of all the mail in the city. This made it easier to circulate the *Gazette*, which in turn brought him even more income.

Being postmaster made circulating
Ben's newspaper even easier

Ben's family was now very comfortable. Deborah gave birth again in 1742 to a daughter they named Sarah. Ben invented a new kind of stove, the Franklin stove, which is still used in some houses today. It provided more heat than a normal stove. Ben made the design available for free so anyone could enjoy or improve on it. His newspaper partners across the colonies helped spread his thoughts and ideas far beyond Pennsylvania. Ben certainly kept working hard, to maintain the reputation he had earned for diligence and quality, and he now embarked on his most famous project yet.

The Franklin Stove was a type of woodburning stove designed to heat a room safely and efficiently and was one of Ben's most popular inventions during his lifetime

Chapter Five
<u>Electricity</u>

Electricity, so important to our modern life, was almost unknown when Ben was young. The only form of electricity recognized in the early 1700s was static electricity, which produces a tiny jolt or shock from friction, or the movement of two forces against each other. When you rub your hands against a thick rug on a dry day and then touch something, the small shock you feel is static electricity. The word *static* means *still*. When Ben was growing up, electricity was hard to study. Scientists had figured out that certain materials, for example, metal, could conduct, or carry, electricity from one place to another. Without a reliable source of electricity to observe, that was as far as they could go.

That changed in 1745, when scientists at the University of Leiden in the Netherlands invented a way to create and trap static electricity. They covered a glass bottle with foil and rotated it around a piece of felt. The resulting friction between the moving foil (a metal) and the felt (a heavy fabric similar to a rug) produced sparks of static electricity. This tool was called a Leiden jar, after the city where it was invented.

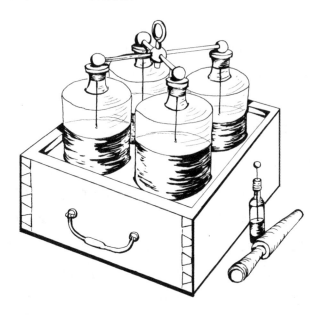

The Leiden Jar trapped static electricity in glass jars and figured into many of Ben's electrical experiments

Suddenly, the great scientific minds of the day could analyze and experiment with electricity. Some of them received bad shocks when they touched metal to a Leiden jar. Ben was lucky enough to have a friend in England, Peter Collinson, send him one in 1746. Fascinated, he started experimenting right away. He brought the Leiden jar to parties and gave himself and friends mild electric shocks. He figured out what materials electricity would attract, and what it would repel. Most importantly, he understood at once that electricity had positive and negative charges, and that within the Leiden jar there could be a high concentration of electricity at one end as well as a total vacuum of electricity at the other.

Ben wrote many letters to Collinson, explaining the advances and discoveries that he had made. In 1749, he found that a pointed metal rod could draw an electric spark from much farther away than a blunt object, and could even repel the electric shock if it had the same charge as the spark. Always on the lookout for a useful project, he wrote to Collinson in July to suggest that long metal rods be placed on top of buildings to protect them from lightning strikes. Many houses at that time were built of wood. Philadelphia in particular was full of row houses, or houses all in a line that shared their side walls with their neighbors. A single spark from a lightning strike could destroy an entire city block. Ben hoped that by repelling electricity, buildings of all kinds could be protected from this kind of damage.

Already he had made the connection between lightning and electricity. Several other experiments proved to him that they had the same effects. If one cloud with a positive charge bumped into another cloud with a negative charge, he reasoned, they would spark in the same way that the electricity in the Leiden jar did—but since clouds are bigger than a Leiden jar, the spark would have to be similarly big. He had also realized that water conducted electricity. (Today, we know that only impure water, like the salt water in the ocean, conducts electricity. But in Ben's time, most available water sources were impure.) No wonder, he thought, that there was so much lightning in a thunderstorm. It was just oppositely charged clouds bumping into each other, surrounded by water!

Finally, he proposed an experiment to test his theory. He suggested putting a pointed iron rod on the top of a steeple, with the lower end near a Leiden jar or another charged tube of glass. If the rod conducted a spark to the glass during a storm, then it would prove that lightning and electricity were one and the same.

This proposed experiment was published in London in 1751, and almost instantly translated into French. Scientists in France scrambled to test Ben's theory. In May of 1752, Thomas-François Dalibard did, in fact, perform Ben's experiment. But before word of Dalibard's success could travel from Paris to Philadelphia, Ben had come up with a better experiment, one that would make him the biggest celebrity in the world.

Flying a kite in a thunderstorm is one of Ben's most memorable experiments and helped him prove lighting and electricity are the same thing

Ben's new experiment came about simply because he was tired of waiting for a tall enough steeple to be built in Philadelphia. He decided that instead of bringing the lightning down to him, he would go up to it. He made a kite and stuck a small pointed metal rod on the very top of it. Then he used silk, which he had found was a good electrical conductor, to tie a key to the kite string near his hand.

On June 15, 1752, a thunderstorm broke over Philadelphia. Ben grabbed the kite and a Leiden jar and ran to the doorway of his house, with 22-year-old William by his side. They stood in the doorway both to protect themselves from lightning and to keep the key and the Leiden jar dry so as not to ruin the experiment. Up went the kite, struggling against the wind. The twine tying the kite together went crazy as the clouds passed over it, each separate filament twisting in a different direction as the fibers reacted to the charged air. Ben reached for the key dancing in the wind. It sparked as his finger approached! He easily passed another spark to the Leiden jar. Breathless with excitement, he reeled in the kite. He had been right—lightning and electricity were the same thing—and he himself had proven it!

Ben received the Copley Medal, a scientific award, in 1752 for his discoveries about electricity

Europe and America greeted Ben's triumph with dazzled awe. Dr. William Watson, one of England's most famous scientists, published a collection of Ben's letters and experiments. Harvard and Yale both awarded him honorary degrees. The Royal Society of London, which was dedicated to science, awarded him the prestigious Copley Medal and made him a member without charging him membership dues. Letters full of praise poured in from across the ocean; Ben exchanged letters with nearly every important scientist in Europe.

Lightning rods became common on American buildings and helped prevent fires caused by lightning strikes

His protective lightning rods were put on houses, on churches, even on ships. They made thousands of invaluable buildings safer than they had ever been. Almost overnight, Ben Franklin was the single American whose name every European knew.

It made him an easy choice when the Pennsylvania Assembly, of which he was now an elected member, needed an ambassador to appeal to England for help against the colony's interfering governors. Because of his celebrity, Ben soon found himself caught between the land of his birth and the empire he saw as the mother country, trying desperately to avoid war between two countries he loved.

Row houses helped save space, but the shared walls meant fires could spread quickly and be more dangerous

Chapter Six
Politics

Of course, Ben hadn't been focusing only on electricity for the last seven years. His experiments were actually just his hobby; he still had a business to run, a family to care for, and public duties to uphold. Both his parents had died, Josiah in 1744 and Abiah a month before the kite experiment, and a grieving Ben had bought a marble stone for their shared grave. Besides, he just couldn't stop coming up with new ideas.

In 1743, when his daughter Sarah was a year old, Ben suggested that Philadelphia create a new kind of college where lessons would be taught in English instead of Latin, and where several experts would handle each topic instead of one teacher trying to do them all.

In 1751, Ben founded the Pennsylvania Hospital with a friend, Dr. Thomas Bond (the hospital still exists today.)

The election of 1753 made him Postmaster General of North America, responsible for mail across all the colonies. In some ways, the really amazing thing about Ben's kite experiment is that he found the time to do it!

Ben helped start a Pennsylvania militia so the colonists could defend themselves during the French and Indian War

With his reputation made, Ben was an indispensable ambassador whenever Pennsylvania needed help. When the French and Indian War broke out in 1754, Ben was sent to Albany, the capital of New

York, to help manage relations between the Indian tribes and the British colonies. Two years later, in the middle of the war, he started a militia so Pennsylvania could defend itself from the threat of a potential attack. He personally raised funds and supplies for the army sent from England to fight the French. He also took part in the militia's basic training and helped to deliver and move the supplies he'd secured. Ben was not only famous, he was also effective. No wonder that in 1757 the Assembly chose him to plead their case against the Penns before the English government.

William Penn, who had founded the colony of Pennsylvania, had died in 1718, five years before Ben would arrive in Philadelphia. After his death, Pennsylvania was governed by his sons and grandsons, many of whom had rejected his modest Quaker beliefs and embraced the aristocracy. Some of them did not even live in Pennsylvania, but in England. They saw the colonies as a hopeless backwater, and much preferred to live in luxury in England, where they could look after their own finances. Although they sent governors to the colony, often these governors had very specific instructions

Parliament is still housed in the same building
as it was in 1757, when Ben saw them,
known as the Houses of Parliament

from the Penns. That made the governors unable to
work with the new laws that the Assembly, which
was made up of elected Pennsylvanians, wanted
to pass. So the fights would go back and forth between the Assembly and the Penns, while nothing
actually changed in the colony.

Ben's job was to go to England and explain to Parliament, the English lawmaking body, that the Penns were making it impossible for the Assembly to do anything. If they were lucky, Parliament might tell the Penns to listen to the Assembly. But since the Penns lived in England, it was unlikely that Parliament would even hear the Assembly's arguments. Ben was the only person who might have a chance to get Parliament's attention. He sailed to England for the second time in 1757. Deborah hated sea travel, so she stayed in Philadelphia to manage the family businesses, and William went with Ben.

The University of St. Andrews, in Scotland, was founded in 1410 and is still operating today

This time, he stayed in England for five years. He traveled to Ecton, where his father had been born, and paid a memorable visit to the University of St. Andrews in Scotland. At last he had the opportunity to speak face-to-face with the scientists he'd shared experiments with by letters. The trip reminded Ben how much he liked England, and how many opportunities it offered that were simply not available in the colonies. But for once his expert political tricks failed him; he returned to Philadelphia in 1762 without completing his mission. He had been celebrated and praised throughout England, and he had won for William the position of Governor of New Jersey, but he had not been able to convince Parliament that the Penns were bad for Pennsylvania.

Back in Philadelphia, Ben took a much more aggressive stance than he ever had before. He had accomplished all his projects by gently coaxing public opinion where he wanted it to go. But now, angry with the Penns and firm in his belief that America needed the protection of England's strength, Ben suggested to the Assembly that they invite Parliament to rule Pennsylvania directly, cutting the Penns out completely. This was one of the few unpopular ideas Ben ever had.

Colonists began to publish pamphlets and flyers questioning the right of England to rule the colonies

To the Assembly, Parliament was even worse than the Penns. Under Parliament's rule, Pennsylvania would still be governed by people an ocean away, but the Assembly would have nowhere to appeal bad decisions. In addition, the American colonies were starting to question the need for English rule at all. Why, they muttered, should they have to obey rules made for them by strangers who'd never set foot in America? Ben lost the next election in 1764, and was out of the Assembly.

The Penns got even worse, and the colonies' dislike of English rule deepened. They wanted to hold office in Parliament, with an equal share in their own government. Again the Assembly needed a voice in England, and there was still only one person to send. Ben went to England for the third time in 1764. This time he would be gone for eleven years, the most momentous decade of his life.

Ben's recent population studies had shown him that Americans were having children much more quickly than the English. America was also much larger, and had many more untapped resources than England. All this had convinced Ben that the American colonies were England's future. He went back to London with that in mind, hopeful that he could make Parliament see what he saw. But Parliament thought of the colonies as a way to make money by taxing them outrageously. Worse, they refused to acknowledge the colonies' issues, thinking instead that because England had supplied America with everything it needed, America should obey England without question.

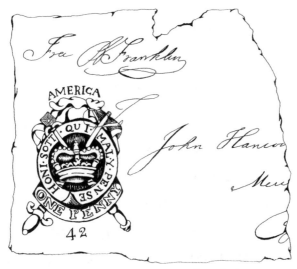

The Stamp Act required any official document, like a bill of sale or deed for a house, to be written on expensive, special paper from London

Ben had many friends and connections in England. He made use of them all to get himself in front of Parliament. But he had very little actual power. All he could do was present his case, advise the lawmakers, and hope that they listened. He found Parliament as unhelpful now as they had been in 1757. They let him speak, but they dismissed his points. In 1765, they even passed the Stamp Act, which required all legal documents in the colonies to be written on stamped paper from London. The taxes on this special paper were high, and it interfered with every aspect of American business. Americans were outraged, and Ben did all he could to stop the Stamp Act, but failed.

Knowing the battle was lost, Ben recommended a friend as Pennsylvania's stamp distributor. When Philadelphia heard of this, the city rioted, thinking that Ben had been in favor of the Stamp Act all along. Deborah had sent Sarah away before the rioting began, but refused to leave herself, although she knew that as Ben's wife she was a target for any unhappy citizens.

On the evening of September 17, as a mob massed in the streets, her cousin Josiah came to the house to protect her; Deborah sent him home to fetch her brother and a gun. When the rioters came that night, Deborah had arranged her relatives along the stairs in defensive formation, and calmly told the mob that since she hadn't done anything wrong, she would not leave her house.

Embarrassed to be threatening a woman, the mob withdrew. Her courage saved Ben's entire livelihood from destruction.

People began displaying a cartoon skull that represented being taxed to death after the Stamp Act

But the colonies' anger at being squeezed for still more money couldn't be so easily defused. Several state Assemblies even declared the Stamp Act unlawful, taking lawmaking initiative completely independent of Parliament. Ben was shocked to hear of this. He had underestimated American dislike for English rule. Now he understood that this was no longer a question of getting Americans into Parliament. Americans didn't want to join England's government; they wanted to be free of England.

To Ben, this was a disaster in the making. Loving America and England, and sure that America was the future of England, he tried even harder to reconcile the two sides. He made a passionate speech against the Stamp Act and helped to undo it. Hearing of this, three other colonies—Massachusetts, New Jersey, and Georgia—made him their spokesman as well.

Ben took this duty very seriously. Although he wanted America and England to stay united, he was already angry at Parliament. Even after the Stamp Act riots, they didn't want to listen to an American perspective. England was one of the strongest countries in the world. Parliament was sure that if the colonies wanted to fight, England could beat them. They thought they had nothing to lose by ignoring America, and nothing to gain by listening.

In London, Ben read the colonists' concerns
and tried to explain them to Parliament

Ben kept talking to them, getting more and more
frustrated. For its part, Parliament soon thought
of Ben not as a peacemaker, but as the ringleader
of the colonies. They even blamed him for the riots
and the unrest, since his was the only voice offering an American opinion. This bad opinion of Ben
came to a head in late 1773, when he had been in
England for nine years.

Perhaps no colony was angrier at Parliament
than Massachusetts, home of Ben's birthplace,

Boston. The Massachusetts Assembly had declared that Parliament had no right to govern the colonies, and had fought with its governor, Thomas Hutchinson. Frustrated, Hutchinson wrote his friends in government in London, urging them to limit the colonists' freedom even more. Since the people of Massachusetts were English citizens, Hutchinson's suggestions weren't exactly legal, but he knew it would be easier to stifle this rebellious anger if Massachusetts residents were denied their rights as citizens.

When Ben discovered these letters, he was shocked. He had thought of Hutchinson as a friend. Maybe, he hoped, if Massachusetts knew that Hutchinson was at fault rather than Parliament, they might be more willing to reconcile with England. He sent Hutchinson's letters to the secretary of the Massachusetts Assembly.

The letters had the opposite effect from what Ben had hoped. They confirmed what the Assembly had suspected: that if the colonies wanted liberty, they were on their own. In the midst of all this, Parliament put a new tax on tea shipped from England.

Colonists, already angry with Parliament, absolutely rejected the new tax and began buying the cheaper, although illegal, tea smuggled in from the Netherlands. In December of 1773, a Boston mob swarmed onto a ship newly arrived from England, overpowered the crew, and threw all the tea on board into the harbor to protest the tea tax.

The Boston Tea Party was a powerful show of rebellion by the colonists as they threw English tea into the Boston harbor

This act of defiance, soon called the Boston Tea Party, was the biggest stance the colonies had ever taken against England. And in London, politicians blamed Ben. He had come to symbolize American resistance to English rule. They could not believe that he hadn't encouraged or even organized the Boston Tea Party, even though he had been in England the whole time. Such an act of rebellion, as they saw it, had to be punished. On January 29, 1774, Parliament met, supposedly to discuss a petition Ben had presented from Massachusetts five months before. In reality, the meeting was a public attack on Ben.

Ben refused to fight back while Parliament
blamed the rebellion on him in 1774

For an hour, Ben stood motionless and silent while Parliament's solicitor general, Alexander Wedderburn, mocked and accused him in front of the very people he had been trying to help. He heard himself called the instigator of all the American unrest and blamed for everything Parliament didn't like. Ben had always refused to defend himself against attack, believing that if he were right, the truth would speak for him. He did the same thing now, letting Wedderburn taunt him as long as he wanted. He saw clearly now that there was no point in trying to change the minds in Parliament. He had spent ten years in England, but never before had it been so clear to him that no one wanted to listen.

Ben resigned as the colonies' agent, but stayed for another year to offer what advice he could. While he was preparing to come home, tragedy struck. Deborah had a stroke in December of 1774, and died two days after Christmas. When Ben finally sailed for Philadelphia in the spring of 1775, he came back to an empty house, a country at war, and a divided family.

The battle of Lexington and Concord, the first of the American Revolution, had taken place while he was traveling. There was no reason, however, to expect that the colonial civilian army could defeat the English military, the best professional army in Europe.

The Battle of Lexington and Concord showed the British army that the Americans were not going to go down without a fight

But the worst was yet to come. Ben's beloved son William, now age forty-five, still held the position of royal governor of New Jersey. As a servant of the King, William had taken the English side and considered anyone who opposed England a traitor. Ben met with William a few weeks after he had arrived in Philadelphia, hoping to win his son over. Instead, trapped on opposite sides by their different loyalties, father and son were soon at each other's throats. Ben and William parted enemies, never to reconcile over the remaining fifteen years of Ben's life.

The American Revolution divided William and Ben, who would never forgive each other

Chapter Seven
Independence

In the midst of war and heartbreak, Ben threw himself into supporting the defiant colonies. As soon as he had landed in Philadelphia, the Pennsylvania Assembly unanimously made him their representative at the Second Continental Congress. This collection of the best and bravest men in the colonies would meet throughout two sweltering Philadelphia summers.

Their original plan was to handle the newly erupted war, but as days turned into months, it became clear that the colonies needed something even bolder than a war. They certainly didn't want to be ruled by England anymore. And if they were no longer English, they must become a new country of their own making, a country that idealists and realists alike could support.

Ben used his old trick of letting other people take the credit. His time in England had convinced him that the sooner the colonies broke with England, the better off they would be. Ben didn't want to be a firebrand, though. Instead he walked a tightrope between extremists and moderates, gently coaxing them all toward his ideal future.

Fifty-six people signed the
Declaration of Independence,
declaring freedom from British rule, in 1776

Finally, in June 1776, the more cautious delegates accepted what Ben already knew: that the colonies' future lay in their own hands, not with England. They put Ben on a committee to write it out. Wisely, the committee let a brilliant young lawyer from Virginia named Thomas Jefferson do most of the work. Jefferson's eloquence and passion were so moving that the committee only made a few small changes to his first draft. In fact, when Jefferson got upset at those changes, it was Ben who cheered him up. On July 4, 1776, the Declaration of Independence was read in public. No longer was Ben an English colonist, but a proud citizen of the brand-new United States of America.

He knew, however, that this was only part of the struggle. They still had a war to win against the best army in the world. With his typical wit, Ben summarized the dangers they faced after the Continental Congress: "We must all hang together," he told the other delegates, "or assuredly we shall all hang separately." Although Ben preferred for the new country to stand on its own, he also knew the reality of America's need. Only with international allies to help fight England did America stand a chance against the strongest military force in Europe. Again Ben's international prestige made him the obvious choice to send on an international errand. In late October, he set sail with his two grandsons (William's son Temple, who had chosen his grandfather over his father, and his daughter Sarah's son who had been named for him) for France, to persuade England's oldest enemy to join the fight on America's side.

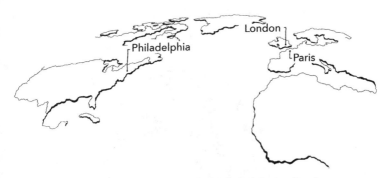

Ben traveled from Philadelphia to Paris,
just 200 miles away from London

Ben was seventy-years old and spoke very bad French, but was as energetic and entertaining as ever. Once again he was eager to be useful, and the fun-loving French court made it easy. Never before had Ben been so celebrated. They put his portrait on plates and trinkets. Nobles and great thinkers begged for a moment of his time. Fashionable ladies clustered around him. Ben was swept up in a whirl of glamour and excitement such as he had never known before.

Amidst all this, Ben never lost sight of his real mission: to make France America's ally. In fact, the French adoration of him made King Louis XVI's ministers take him very seriously. Cleverly, Ben played to the French image of him as a humble genius from a

Ben tried to appear humble by wearing
a fur cap and common clothes instead
of the dramatic fashion of the aristocracy

rustic backwater. He had his portrait painted wearing a fur cap like an ordinary country fellow, and took care not to wear the rare and expensive fabrics of the French court. He knew that this would make the French think even better of him for resisting the temptation of elegance.

Unfortunately, making an alliance wasn't as easy as wearing plain clothes. America had just signed the Declaration of Independence a few months before Ben arrived in Paris. Although France certainly wanted England to look bad, they weren't willing to risk an open alliance with America before they knew that America wouldn't simply be crushed by England. Caution was certainly wise from the French point of view, but Ben knew that without French help, America would have no way of sustaining an army of any size. England had supported the colonies; without trade with England to bring in money and much-needed supplies, America was in real trouble.

Even worse, America itself wasn't sure if it was one single nation or thirteen loosely connected states. While Ben was asking the French for loans of money, several states had representatives in Paris asking for the same thing to mount militias and local defense forces for those particular states, rather than for George Washington's Continental Army. How could Ben reassure the French that America had a promising future when no one knew for certain what America even was?

France's King Louis XVI was unsure about supporting the colonies, but Ben convinced him

A social man himself, Ben soon realized how French politics worked. The French court lived by a rigorous and exhaustive set of rules, or etiquette, that dictated everything from seating arrangements at dinners to the names and ranks of courtiers privileged enough to watch King Louis XVI wake up and wash his face. Only five years before Ben's arrival in France, Queen Marie Antoinette had caused a year-long scandal by refusing to speak to the previous king's mistress. By the rules of etiquette, the mistress could not speak to a higher-ranking person first. Even with all his experience with Parliament and the Pennsylvania Assembly, Ben had never before encountered a world quite like this.

Ben was nothing if not quick-witted. He understood that in such a formal, rigidly defined world, he would never accomplish anything if he got straight to business. Besides, although the French ministers wanted to weaken England, they preferred to do so secretly at first. Since Ben was a traitor in English eyes, he couldn't arrange a formal meeting without forcing the French to show their hand and making the French angry with him. Instead of presenting his case, as he had hoped to do in Parliament, Ben jumped into the whirl of court pastimes: dances, dinner parties, late-morning teas and card games that lasted until dawn. All the important ministers attended such events, and Ben's celebrity made them curious to meet him even before he worked his charm on them.

Much of Ben's work was done at social events like dances, parties, or dinners

Ben knew that people bound by such rules wanted more than anything to have fun. So he made sure to be charming and amusing, cracking jokes and bantering with the best. Soon word got around that the American ambassador was the life of the party. Courtiers who got to know Ben as a person rather than as an envoy offered much more assistance to their new friend than they ever would have to a foreign beggar.

Ben recognized the power that aristocratic ladies held in the French court and made sure to befriend as many of them as he could

He also took special care to befriend several intelligent and highly-placed ladies at court. Both he and they knew that his outrageous flirtations weren't meant to be taken seriously. Being "court-ed" by the famous Ambassador Franklin only cemented the witty reputations of the ladies and

the ladies were happy to urge their powerful relatives to support Ben's cause.

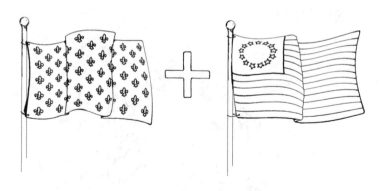

France and America's alliance was
the key to winning the war

Winning France to America's side was a job that
no one else could have done. Ben did it by play-
ing the game of politics, by using his own fame
to represent his young country, and by sincerely
appreciating the diplomatic and monetary risks
that France was taking by supporting America. Often he had to do this in the face of attacks from
other Americans, who thought he was really serv-
ing France's interests and not theirs when he didn't
fulfill their every demand.

Congress meant to make things easier on seven-
ty-two-year-old Ben by sending John Adams to Paris
to help him. Instead, Adams made things worse.

Adams had many good qualities, including loyalty, intelligence, and perseverance. But he was easily offended if he didn't think he was valued enough. He was a terrible choice for ambassador, and his methods clashed with Ben's.

Adams thought that Ben spent too much time in pointless small talk, completely oblivious to the fact that France had only given America money because of its respect and admiration for Ben. Small talk and dinner parties were Ben's political weapons of choice. Adams was bad at both.

Adams wasn't just inept in social situations. He cornered the French foreign minister, the Count de Vergennes, and bluntly asked for more money, men, and supplies. Ben had worked hard to befriend Vergennes; when the Count told Ben about the confrontation with Adams, Ben was furious. Adams's abrupt treatment of Vergennes had put the alliance in danger. In order to do his job, Ben had to ask Congress to bring Adams home.

With Adams out of the way, Ben could work his magic on France. In spite of enemies at home, interference in Paris, and France running low on

Ben met with King Louis XVI and Marie Antoinette and convinced them that France should ally with America

money, Ben kept them on America's side. French help proved crucial to several major battles, but none as important as the Battle of Yorktown in the fall of 1781. No sooner had the English general, Charles Cornwallis, stationed his army in the city of Yorktown, Virginia, than a French fleet blockaded the port and trapped the English army in American territory. General George Washington and the French general Rochambeau marched their army south and pinned Cornwallis by land as well as by sea. Finally, after more than six long years of war,

Cornwallis surrendered to Washington on October 19, 1781.

America had won independence, but Ben's work was far from over. He had negotiated the alliance with France. Now, at age seventy-seven, Ben was the only choice to work out a permanent treaty between victorious America and France and defeated England. More than ever, tact and delicacy were crucial. A successful treaty must pave the way for America's international future, as well as rewarding France for its help. Ben also believed that if America and England were ever going to be friends again, England must be truly apologetic for its part in the war.

Congress sent a peacemaking team to Paris to help Ben. Unfortunately, they included Adams in that team. On the other hand, the chief English negotiator, the Earl of Shelburne, was an old friend of Ben's. After months of discussion, the borders of the United States were formally established, and the Treaty of Paris was signed on September 3, 1783. While some of Ben's proposals (such as the idea of England offering America its Canadian territory)

The Treaty of Paris was signed by John Jay, John Adams, Benjamin Franklin, Ben's grandson William Temple Franklin, and Henry Laurens

didn't go through, the treaty did establish peace and future relations for the United States with both France and England. Most importantly, from Ben's point of view, it brought a long-awaited end to the war and a promising future for his young country.

As Ben saw it, he had been one of many hard-working people who had helped America gain its independence. The rest of the world saw things differently. Especially in France, people thought Ben was the only man responsible for the creation of

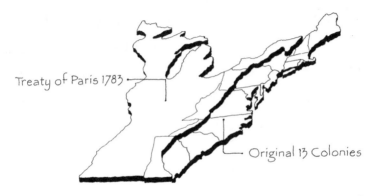

The Treaty of Paris gave France the large tract of land on the other side of the Appalachian Mountains while giving the colonies their own land as well

the United States. He was overwhelmed with letters asking help, recommendations, and money. Congress still relied on him for French support. Adams still thought Ben was conspiring against him, which Ben was afraid would make France unwilling to lend America any more money.

Although Ben still liked to be praised and admired for his accomplishments, he also felt the weight of his age. He had far outlived most of his peers, and he was often sick with gout. His eyesight was weak enough that he needed two pairs of glasses, and had to switch between them for reading or for seeing things at a distance. This became so frustrating that in 1784 he cut the lenses of both glasses in half and put one half of each lens in the same frame. These new double-vision glasses were called bifocals and are another of Ben's inventions that are still used today.

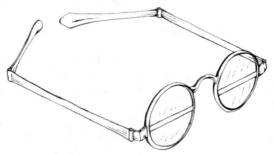

Bifocals, created for Ben's convenience, are one of his inventions still used today

Although his mind was as sharp as ever, Ben was tired. He had loved his time in France, but he wanted to come home to the country he had helped build. Finally, in 1785, Congress recalled him. Ben was held in such high esteem at court that Queen Marie Antoinette lent him her own carriage to carry him on board his ship home.

Chapter Eight
<u>Legacy</u>

Ben arrived home for the last time on September 13, 1785, after nearly nine years in France. Crowds lined the wharf to welcome their local hero and spoke of him in the same breath as George Washington. A month after his return, he was unanimously elected president of Pennsylvania, and

Ben, a national hero, finally got to spend
time with his daughter and her family
after returning from Paris in 1785

reelected for two more years, which was the longest anyone could serve at that time. Luckily, the most he had to do as president was to sign papers. At last Ben could relax and take a long-deserved vacation. His daughter Sarah and her family lived nearby; he could visit them as often as he wanted, and finally enjoy the kind of quiet life he had never led.

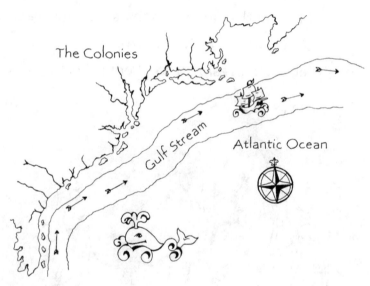

The Gulf Stream, first noticed by Ben, is an ocean current that helps ships sail to Europe faster

He also kept on inventing devices to make life easier. He designed a tool to get books off shelves too high to reach. He hosted meetings of the

American Philosophical Society, which had begun with the Junto, and presented to them the research he had done in England on what we know today as the Gulf Stream. Ben was the first person to chart it, as well as giving it its name. His old friends in England still valued his thoughts and insights, in spite of the war. Although in theory he had retired, in reality he was as sharp and curious as ever, and loved to keep himself thinking.

His fellow Americans couldn't do without him. It was clear that America's first system of government, the Articles of Confederation, wasn't working. In May of 1787, the Constitutional Convention met in Philadelphia. Ben was eighty-one and very sick, but an essential presence all the same. He had to be carried in a chair to the meeting place, which is now Philadelphia's Independence Hall. He attended every meeting for four months through yet another blazing summer. Not only did he want to have a say in the shaping of the government, but he also knew that without him there to lend symbolic approval, the new Constitution wouldn't be well received in America or abroad. Ben became one of only six

Founding Fathers to sign both the Declaration of Independence and the United States Constitution.

Though he had to be carried there in a chair, Ben attended all of the Constitutional Convention's meetings as a show of support for the new government

Even after the Constitution was ratified, Ben kept busy. Although as a younger man he had kept a slave, he had been convinced for many years that slavery was wrong. In 1789, he published essays arguing for abolition, or the end of slavery, and in 1790 he became the president of the newly founded Pennsylvania Abolition Society. Sadly, he didn't have much time left to fight slavery as he had fought for America. On April 17, 1790, he died of pleurisy, or an inflammation of the lungs. He was buried at Christ Church in Philadelphia, next to Deborah.

At the time of his death, Ben was eighty-four years old. Sarah and her eight children survived him, including his namesake who had been with him in France. Ben had kept in touch with his sister Jane

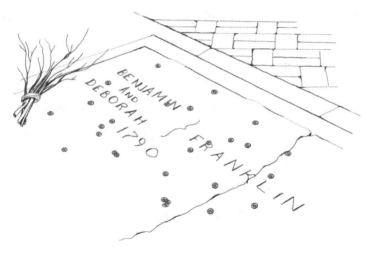

People still show their respect by throwing pennies on Ben's grave as a nod to his saying "a penny saved is a penny earned" from *Poor Richard's Almanac*

for his entire life, offering sympathy, advice and money as she struggled to make ends meet, so she lost not only a beloved brother, but also a protector and financial supporter. Now in England, William also survived Ben, as did his thirty-year-old son Temple, who had helped him so much in France and had been with Ben at the moment of his death.

Ben's will provided particularly for the members of his family who needed the most help. He had bought his parents' Boston house, where Jane still lived. In his will he not only gave her sixty pounds per year, but he also willed her the house to give her some stability.

Ben had always hoped that Congress would employ his grandson Temple in gratitude for Temple's help in France; they never did, so Ben left Temple money, land in Georgia, and most of Ben's books and papers. These included his unfinished autobiography, which Temple edited and published in 1816. It is one of the first American autobiographies, making Ben a pioneer even beyond the grave. Ben left most of his estate to Sarah and her children. Forward-thinking until the end, he left a thousand pounds each to the cities of Boston and Philadelphia, which he intended to gather interest over at least a hundred years and then be spent on projects to benefit each city. Both these bequests grew hugely, and were spent in the 20th century: Philadelphia's on scholarships for students in need of financial help, and Boston's on the creation of the Franklin Institute of Technology.

Ben was buried next to his wife in the graveyard of Christ Church in Philadelphia in 1790

The nation mourned along with Ben's family. At his funeral on April 21, 1790, the men who walked to Christ Church with Ben's coffin included Philadelphia's mayor, Samuel Powel, and Ben's friend

A statue of Ben sits inside the
University of Pennsylvania, honoring his
achievements and dedication

and fellow scientist, David Rittenhouse. 20,000 Philadelphians joined the funeral procession; at that time, the city's population was 28,000. The city's flags flew at half-mast in tribute. James Madison asked the House of Representatives to wear mourning for a month in Ben's honor. In France, whose 1789 Revolution had been inspired by America's, the National Assembly sent eulogies of Franklin across the sea to Congress.

Ben had set out to be useful, and had ended up helping to build a nation. His scientific discoveries changed the world as he knew it. He had faced dozens of personal challenges and sorrows, and had survived them by devoting himself to service. Ben Franklin had become, in his own lifetime, one of the two most admired and revered Americans in the world.

His legacy endures to this day. Several of the institutions he founded still thrive, like the Library Company and the University of Pennsylvania. Lightning rods still protect buildings from burning down. Colleges, bridges, medals, and fictional characters have been named in his honor. Thanks to his funny and engaging writing, his own account of his life has become one of the great examples of autobiography. Thousands of people rely on bifocals to help them see. In 1928, as a testament of gratitude for his decades of work, the United States put his portrait on the $100 bill. Ben's passion, creativity, and vision make some scholars call him "the first American."

Benjamin Franklin is honored with a place on our national currency. He is on the $100 bill

But Ben wouldn't have thought of himself that way. All the acclaim might even have embarrassed him. For Ben, who spent his life trying to make things better, the best legacy he could have imagined would be that we still use his inventions, value his insights, and work to sustain and improve the country he helped shape.

Select Quotes from
<u>Ben Franklin</u>

"A stitch in time saves nine."
  – on the benefits of doing important tasks right away

"A friend in need is a friend indeed."
  – on true friendship

"Fish and visitors stink after three days."
  – poking fun at guests who stay too long

"As we enjoy great advantages from the inventions of others, we should be glad of an opportunity to serve others by any invention of ours, and this we should do freely and generously."
  – explaining his refusal to make money off his inventions

"We must all hang together, or assuredly we shall all hang separately."
  – after the signing of the Declaration of Independence

Ben Franklin's Life Timeline

1706 Born in Boston

1718 Apprenticed to his brother James

1721 James founds the *New England Courant*; Ben starts writing the Silence Dogood letters

1722 Takes over the paper when James is jailed

1723 Runs away from Boston and goes to Philadelphia

1724 Sails to London

1726 Returns to Philadelphia and goes back to Keimer

1727 Creates the Junto

1728 Sets up a printing house with Hugh Meredith

1729 Takes over the *Pennsylvania Gazette*

1730 Ben and Deborah marry and first son, William is born

1731 William is born

1732 Begins to publish *Poor Richard's Almanac*; Francis Franklin born in October

1736 Creates the Union Fire Company, and prints New Jersey currency using anti-counterfeiting techniques he devised; Francis dies of smallpox

1741 Invents the Franklin stove

1742 Sarah Franklin born

1743 Founds the American Philosophical Society

1749 Named president of the Academy and College; elected Philadelphia Justice of the Peace

1751 Elected to Pennsylvania Assembly

World Timeline

1707   The Acts of Union join England and Scotland into one kingdom

1714   George I becomes King of England, beginning the Hanover dynasty

1718   French writer and philosopher Voltaire first adopts this pseudonym

1722   The Three Years War starts in Maine between colonists and Native Americans

1727   The colonies experience their first earthquake on record; many are injured

1729   South Carolina becomes a colony

1732   James Oglethorpe founds the colony of Georgia

1745   Scientists in the Netherlands invent the Leiden jar

1749   Ohio becomes an English territory and settlers begin exploring the Ohio valley

1751   Pennsylvania Hospital, is formed

Ben Franklin's Life Timeline (cont.)

1752   Performs kite experiment with William assisting

1753   Receives Copley Medal from the Royal Society

1755   Franklin's College of Philadelphia opens

1757   Sent to England by the Pennsylvania Assembly to protest the power of the Penn family

1764   Loses his seat in the October Assembly elections, and is sent again to London

1765   Testifies against the Stamp Act in Commons

1774   Ben's wife Deborah dies

1775   Arrives in Philadelphia, and is unanimously chosen by the Pennsylvania Assembly as their delegate to the Second Continental Congress; breaks with William

1776   Chosen for the Committee of Five that draws up the Declaration of Independence

1778   Negotiates alliance between US and France

1784   Invents bifocals

1785   Elected president of Pennsylvania

1787   Signs Constitution of the United States

1788   Finishes his autobiography

1790   Becomes president of the Pennsylvania Abolition Society

1790   Dies in Philadelphia, and is buried there

World Timeline (cont.)

1760   King George II dies; George III becomes King of England

1762   Catherine the Great becomes Empress of Russia

1763   The French and Indian War ends

1763   Seven-year-old Wolfgang Amadeus Mozart begins his grand tour of Europe

1765   The Stamp Act is passed

1764   The phrase "No Taxation without Representation" begins showing up around the colonies

1773   Boston Tea Party

1774   The First Continental Congress meets in Philadelphia"

1775   The Battle of Lexington and Concord begins the American Revolution

1775   The Second Constitutional Convention opens

1775   Louis XVI and Marie Antoinette become King and Queen of France

1776   Congress ratifies the Declaration of Independence

1781   The English general, Lord Cornwallis, surrenders to George Washington at the Battle of Yorktown, ending the American Revolution

1783   The American Revolution ends with the signing of the Treaty of Paris

1787   The Constitutional Convention begins in Philadelphia

1790   George Washington delivers the first State of the Union Address

Glossary

Almanac   A handbook, published every year, containing useful information like weather forecasts and calendars

Ambassador   A person sent to represent his or her homeland and its interests in a foreign country

American Revolution   The war fought between England and its American colonies between 1776 and 1783, in which America's victory secured its independence from England

Apprentice   An unpaid person who works alongside a master for a set number of years in order to learn the master's trade

Aristocracy   An upper class that is usually based on birth and is richer and more powerful than the rest of society

Autobiography   A person's life story, as told by themselves; Ben Franklin's autobiography is one of the classics of the genre

Bifocals   Glasses invented by Ben Franklin in 1784 with double lenses that allow the wearer to see things up close and far away

Boston   The capital city of the Massachusetts colony, and the site of Ben Franklin's birth and childhood; later the site of the Boston Tea Party on December 16, 1773

Colony   A territory ruled by another country, and subject to that country's laws

Constitution   The law of the United States and one of its founding documents, drafted in 1787 at the Constitutional Convention in Philadelphia; Ben Franklin was one of its thirty-nine signers

Constitutional Convention   The meeting of fifty-five delegates in Philadelphia in 1787, at which the Constitution was drafted from May to September

Courtier   A person who attends to a ruler at a royal court, usually aristocrats

Declaration of Independence   The document, written by Thomas Jefferson, in which the colonies rejected English rule and formed a new country, the United States. Ben Franklin was part of the five-member committee that edited the Declaration, as well as being one of its fifty-six signers

Delegate   A person sent to a meeting (such as Congress) to represent a specific group of people and their needs

Dowry   Money that a woman brings to her husband in a marriage

Franklin Stove   A stove Ben Franklin invented in 1741, designed to distribute heat more evenly throughout the room and make cooking easier

Governor   A person chosen by the government to lead a specific place like a colony or state

Junto   The society formed by Ben Franklin to promote public service, clever thinking, and good writing

Leiden Jar   A tool for creating static electricity, invented in the Dutch city of Leiden in 1745

New England Courant   The newspaper founded by James Franklin in 1721, for which Ben Franklin wrote the Silence Dogood letters

Pennsylvania Gazette   The newspaper founded by William Keimer in 1728 and bought by Ben Franklin in 1729

Persona   A personality assumed by an author in a written work

Printing Press   A complicated piece of technology used to print everything from newspapers to books to drawings

Pseudonym   A false name used by someone who doesn't want their writing to be recognized; Ben Franklin's most famous pseudonyms were Silence Dogood and Richard Saunders

Puritans   People who were part of a religious group that opposed many of the Church of England's teachings and customs. They had very strict moral rules and mostly existed in the 16th and 17th centuries

Quaker   A version of Christianity that believes in equality and pacifism, or not fighting

Ratify   To make something official

Second Continental Congress   A meeting of delegates from the original thirteen colonies in Philadelphia that managed the war effort from 1775 to 1781; Ben Franklin served as Pennsylvania's delegate and helped to draft the Declaration of Independence

Static Electricity   A form of electricity contained in one place, such as inside a Leiden jar

Tallow   The animal fat used to make non-wax candles

Treaty of Paris   The treaty between France, England, and the United States that established France as America's ally and laid out the terms of peace between all three countries; Ben Franklin helped to negotiate it, as well as having signed it

Bibliography

Franklin, Benjamin. *The Autobiography of Benjamin Franklin.* Boston: Bedford/St. Martin's, 2003.

Franklin, Benjamin. *The Papers of Benjamin Franklin.* http://franklinpapers.org/franklin//Packard Humanities Institute, 2006

Morgan, Edmund S. *Benjamin Franklin.* New Haven: Yale University Press, 2002.

Scott, Anne Firor. "Self-Portraits: Three Women." *Making the Invisible Woman Visible.* Champaign: University of Illinois Press, 1984.

Further Reading

Asimov, Isaac. *The Kite That Won the Revolution.* Boston: Houghton Mifflin, 2000.

Fleming, Candace. *Ben Franklin's Almanac: Being a True Account of the Good Gentleman's Life.* New York: Atheneum, 2003.

Fleming, Candace. *The Hatmaker's Sign.* New York: Scholastic, 2000.

Lawson, Robert. *Ben and Me.* New York: Little, Brown and Company, 1988.

Index